SAXON

ENGLAND

SAXON
ENGLAND

TEXT BY JOHN HAMILTON

DRAWINGS BY ALAN SORRELL

Philadelphia
Dufour Editions
1968

Published in the United States 1968
by Dufour Editions, Inc. Chester Springs. Pennsylvania 19425

In the same series
ROMAN BRITAIN

Text by Aileen Fox
Drawings by Alan Sorrell

Library of Congress Catalog Card Number: 68-25985

PRINTED IN GREAT BRITAIN FOR DUFOUR EDITIONS

CONTENTS

The jacket picture shows a Saxon ship burial. The coins shown on the half-title are of Offa and Alfred. The helmet on the title-page and the buckle on page 48 are from the Sutton Hoo treasure: the originals are of gold.
The drawings of Mawgan Porth on pages 42-43 are based on drawings by Alan Sorrell which are the property of the Ministry of Public Building and Works. The drawings of a Viking farmstead and village on pages 40-41 are based on drawings by Alan Sorrell published in The Illustrated London News, *and are reproduced by courtesy of the Editor.*

SOME OTHER BOOKS
ABOUT SAXON ENGLAND

R. H. Hodgkin, *A History of the Anglo-Saxons* (3rd edition Oxford 1952) provides an excellent, well-illustrated history of the period.

R. G. Collingwood and J. N. L. Myres, *Roman Britain and the English Settlements* (Oxford 1936) and F. M Stenton, *Anglo-Saxon England* (Oxford 1943) are authoritative works on the early and later periods respectively providing extensive bibliographies.

The society and beliefs of the early period are described in H. M. Chadwick, *The Origin of the English Nation* (Cambridge 1907), and *Studies in Anglo-Saxon Institutions* (Cambridge 1935).

Weapons, sculpture, jewellery, pottery, churches and manuscripts are well illustrated in G. Baldwin Brown, *The Arts in Early England* (six volumes 1903-37), in British Museum, *Guide to Anglo-Saxon and Foreign Teutonic Antiquities* (1923), and in T. D. Kendrick, *Anglo-Saxon to A.D. 900* (1938), and *Late Saxon and Viking Art*.

The archaeology of the period has been recently reviewed by D. M. Wilson, *The Anglo-Saxons* (1960), H. Arbman, *The Vikings* (1961), and J. Brondsted, *The Vikings* (1960). Social aspects of the scene are vividly portrayed by D. Whitelock, *The Beginnings of English Society* (Pelican 1952).

For those who wish to read original sources in translation recent publications include *The Anglo-Saxon Chronicle* (Tr. Garmonsway, Everyman's Library, 1955), *Bede, A History of the English Church and People* (Penguin 1955), *Beowulf* (Tr. J. R. Clark Hall 1950), R. K. Gordon's anthology *Anglo-Saxon Poetry* (Everyman's Library 1926), and D. Whitelock, *English Historical Documents 500-1042* (1955).

Publications of the English Place-Name Society and the Ordnance Survey Maps of Dark Age Britain are invaluable to those interested in local history and field antiquities.

1. *Saxon raiders landing on the east coast. Each boat, over 70 feet in length, could carry a complement of 40 persons. The Roman signal tower is of the type in use between 370 and 395 along the Yorkshire coast.*

ROMAN AND SAXON

IN THE FOURTH CENTURY the Roman province of Britain offered a rich source of plunder to the Picts and Scots who lived beyond its northern and western frontiers, as well as to Saxon pirates from across the North Sea. Despite the building by the Romans of the " Saxon shore " forts extending from the Wash to the Solent, these marauders over-ran the eastern half of the province in A.D. 367-8.

In the ensuing years a chain of signal stations was built along the Yorkshire coast, and improved naval tactics were introduced. The die, however, was cast. The defence of the Roman Empire against the barbarians called for the progressive withdrawal of troops from Britain, and, as elsewhere, increasing use had to be made of mercenaries

7

2.   *At the end of the Roman period many villas were abandoned by their owners and allowed to fall into decay.   Few were settled by the Saxons except by squatters, the newcomers preferring their own timber frame farmsteads closer to arable fields and pasture.*

(*foederati*) to man the defences and to maintain the garrisons of the eastern towns. Saxon and Frisian spearmen were among these mercenaries, as is apparent from the discovery of Romano-Saxon pottery on such sites as Colchester, Lincoln, York, Cambridge and

Chesterford. Eventually, it proved impossible to maintain a centralized army command in Britain, and in A.D. 410 the Emperor Honorius in a letter addressed to the chief cities of the province told them that they must look after themselves.

History is silent on the measures the Romano-Britons adopted for their own defence, but it would appear from the traditions preserved by later chroniclers that regional commanders arose who were responsible for the organization of military resistance in

9

their areas. In the north we hear of Cunedda, possibly of Pictish descent, whose father and grandfather bore Roman names. Cunedda and his sons are reported to have driven the Irish Scots out of North Wales, and most of the later Welsh dynasties down to the Norman Conquest traced their descent from him. Other prominent leaders or kings were Coelhen in Northern Yorkshire and the borders, Caradoc at Caerwent, Constantine in Somerset, Devon and Cornwall, Ambrosius in the South and most important of all Vortigern (his name means 'overlord') whose seat was in eastern Wales but whose power extended over south-east Britain.

It was Vortigern, so legend relates, who employed Saxon mercenaries under the leadership of Hengist and Horsa in the eastern part of the land to repel the repeated devastations of the Picts and Scots. These Saxon companies, expanded by reinforcements from the homeland, turned upon the Britons, who were forced to cede a large area comprising present-day Essex, Middlesex and Sussex. Horsa was killed in battle, and Hengist became the conqueror of all south-east Britain about A.D. 450.

THE CONTINENTAL HOMELAND

The region from which the invaders came — the Danish peninsula, Slesvig and the North German plain between the Elbe and the Weser — had been occupied by Germanic tribes since the Early Iron Age. The Roman writer Tacitus gives us a remarkably vivid picture of their social organization and customs in the first century A.D. In the centuries preceding the migration the social and political pattern underwent considerable change with the emergence of new confederacies. Among the Angli of central and eastern Jutland power was concentrated in royal dynasties and their courts (gesithas), who played a leading part in the invasion of Britain. To the south other tribes combined in a Saxon confederacy (Saxon is a group name meaning 'men of the Seax', or short sword, like the Franks or 'spearmen') whose power eventually extended through Frisia to the mouths of the Rhine. The aristocratic nature of society in the heroic age is well portrayed in the English epic poem *Beowulf*, which tells of the exploits of Danish and Swedish kings in the 5th and 6th centuries. They are seen feasting in great timber halls surrounded by their noble companions, retainers, minstrels, womenfolk and slaves.

Further light has been thrown upon everyday life and the seafaring habits of the Germanic tribes by archaeological discoveries in their old homeland. At Nydam in the

3.   *Warendorf, near Munster, is one of the most extensive Saxon settlements excavated in the continental homeland.   The largest dwellings, over 80 feet in length, were constructed of timber with thatched roofs, daub-coated walls and porches.   Smaller outhouses, byres, stables and hay-. stack bases were associated with the main farmsteads.*

territory of the Angli, an oak boat similar to those employed in the harrying of the Roman coastal stations has been found preserved in a peat bog. Over 70 feet in length, less than 11 feet wide and with 14 oars on either side it must have easily eluded the clumsier and heavier Roman galleys. Some forty people could be packed into the boat. Close by were their weapons — more than five hundred spears with ash shafts, 8 to 10 feet in length, swords, wooden bows, iron and bone tipped arrows, and round wooden shields.

In another peat bog at Thorsbjerg the body of a warrior was discovered, together with his well-preserved clothing, which included a finely woven long-sleeved tunic, trousers fastened round the waist by a belt, with short stockings attached to the trouser legs. A large square woollen cloak with long fringes had been worn over his shoulders, and leather sandals or Roman pattern had once adorned his feet.

Within recent years several settlements have been excavated. At Warendorf, near Munster in Germany, a whole village has been uncovered. The dwellings were rectangular wooden frame buildings, the largest measuring 80 feet by 21 feet, with porches, wattle and daub walls, and thatched roofs. Numerous barns, stables, byres, as well as hay-stack bases were associated with the farmsteads. Seed recovered showed that crops included barley, oats and wheat. Flax was grown for cloth making, and woad for dyeing.

The calendar used by such agricultural communities was a solar one based upon the solstices and equinoxes. The unceasing round of farming activities is reflected in the later Scandinavian names of the months. Thus spring sowing took place in April-May (Saðtið), lambing in May-June (Stekktið), the hay harvest was gathered in July-August (Heyannir), the corn cut in August-September (Kornskurðarmánuðr), the killing off of surplus livestock for winter provision either by salting or drying occurred in October-November (Gormánuðr) while the mid-winter feasts were held in Hrutmánuðr (December-January) preceding the lean months of the year (Thorri and Goi). In the version introduced to Britain the early spring months were dedicated to ancient fertility goddesses Hretha and Eostre, the latter giving us our name for Easter; May was Trimilci when cows were milked three times daily. As in the homeland November (Blótmánath) saw the sacrifice or slaughter of surplus livestock.

PAGAN BELIEFS

The pagan deities Tiw, Odin (Woden), Thor, Frey and Freya worshipped by the early Teutonic tribes are sky and fertility gods of great antiquity whose veneration is still commemorated in our weekday names. Tiw, like Zeus, was the Indo-European sky or sun god. Odin (Woden) the one-eyed god of wisdom, was also the cunning god of war whose cult appealed to the warrior class. Thor the god of lightning, whose symbol was the hammer or axe, was the protector of the humbler farmer and peasant. Freya was a fertility goddess who, like the goddess Nerthus described by Tacitus, was taken about the countryside in a waggon to receive offerings and to bless the crops. That the worship of these pagan deities was introduced into Britain by the Anglo-Saxons is evident from the widespread occurrence of their names — Tysoe, Tuesley, Wodneslawe, Wednesbury,

Wansdyke — in these and other places. Heathen sanctuaries containing wooden idols or effigies of the gods were set up in forest clearings and on hill tops. Many became the meeting place of the later administrative courts, while others, after the conversion, were consecrated in the name of the church. An East Anglian king in the seventh century, for instance, remembered seeing as a boy an altar to Christ being set up beside the old gods in such a shrine.

Belief in an after life was universal and the dead, whether cremated or interred, were accompanied by grave goods. Women were buried with their treasured personal possessions, brooches, chatelaines and workboxes; the men with their spears, shields, and swords. Often a wife or a slave accompanied the dead to the grave. Cremation was particularly widespread among many of the immigrant tribes and was accompanied by considerable ritual. In many instances the dead were placed in a mortuary house resembling a timber cone piled with brushwood (fig. 4). Gifts were placed by the corpse and the last obsequies paid before the pyre was lit. Beowulf was burned inside such a pyre, as were many of the Scandinavian kings of the Migration period. After the embers had cooled the ashes were carefully searched for bone fragments, which were then placed in a funerary urn (fig. 5) and buried in a mound or small pit in an urn cemetery. In England, as on the Continent, many of the urns were specially made for this purpose, being finer ware, decorated with bosses, incised lines and stamps, than the ordinary everyday pottery made by the womenfolk in the settlements.

Few funeral practices, however, could exceed in ritual and wealth the famous royal ship burials recorded from the Migration period in Sweden, from the seventh century at Sutton Hoo in East Anglia, and from the Viking period in Norway and Russia. The Sutton Hoo burial, attributed to a king of the Wuffingas whose body was lost in battle about A.D. 660, produced the richest treasure ever found in Britain. It included household silver, personal jewellery and weapons ornamented in gold and silver as well as the royal regalia. Following the conversion, grave goods disappear except in the case of kings and of ecclesiastical dignatories like St. Cuthbert who was interred with his pectoral cross, portable altar, comb, and gospel book.

THE SETTLEMENT

The rebellion of the Saxon mercenaries in south-east Britain was followed by the

The lighting of a timber funeral pyre erected over a dead warrior. After the ceremony funeral games were held, as described in "Beowulf"

large scale settlement of colonists who began to arrive in ever-increasing numbers from about the middle of the fifth century. It has been estimated that as many as 15,000 to 20,000 emigrated from the province of Angul, while a further 80,000 to 100,000 probably came from the neighbouring Saxon territories.

The main force of the invasion in its initial stage was directed to the eastern counties north of the Thames, where numerous large cemeteries occur dating to the fifth century. Penetrating inland from the shelving Norfolk coast the settlers established a kingdom in

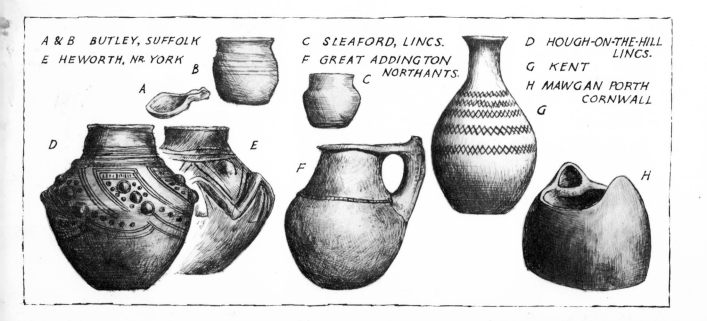

A & B BUTLEY, SUFFOLK
E HEWORTH, NR. YORK

C SLEAFORD, LINCS.
F GREAT ADDINGTON NORTHANTS.

D HOUGH-ON-THE-HILL LINCS.
G KENT
H MAWGAN PORTH CORNWALL

East Anglia, perhaps with the active participation of rebellious mercenaries at Caister-by-Norwich (Venta Icenorum), for the genealogy of their royal family (the Wuffingas) traced their descent from a Roman Emperor. It was this family who buried the famous ship and treasure at Sutton Hoo in the seventh century. Other settlers pressed further inland and settled in the area around Cambridge, which for a time seems to have served as the capital of a Middle Anglian kingdom, the forerunner of Mercia. The leader of these settlers was probably Eomer (he is mentioned in *Beowulf*) whose family name Icelingas is preserved in many place names in the district. The later

5. *Saxon pottery: A, B, C, domestic wares; D, E, cinerary urns; F, handled jug; G, Kentish flask-shaped bottle; H, bar-lip pot.*

6. *Saxon settlers: the men wore trousers, three-quarter-length tunic and cape. Women's dress included a longer tunic and cloak with hood.*

Mercian kings include him in their king list as a descendant of Offa, the son of Wermund the Wise, who ruled in Denmark about the middle of the fourth century. Cemeteries and place-names show that the Anglo-Saxon penetration of the Midlands was by way of the river systems of the Ouse, Cam, Nene and Welland valleys, as well as westward from the Cambridge region to the Upper Thames. Kent, too, received many settlers.

7. Artorius was probably a successful commander of a mobile army in which cavalry played an important part. In medieval romance he emerges as King Arthur.

The settlement of southern England is less clear. According to later tradition the invaders were led by Cerdic, who landed at the head of Southampton Water. Cerdic, however, is a Celtic name, and no conclusive evidence has been found to support the claim. Indeed, the earliest cemeteries in Wessex and their associated grave goods argue for the continued penetration of settlers who had reached the Upper Thames valley from the Cambridge and East Anglian area. It is significant that the genealogy of the West Saxon kings traces their descent from Wig and Freawine, who were Anglian prefects in Slesvig under Wermund the Wise.

It was in this south-western region that the Anglo-Saxons, according to later writers, met with stubborn resistance from the Romano-Britons, led first by Ambrosius Aurelius

about A.D. 470-80 and later by Artorius, the King Arthur of medieval legend. The great earthwork known as the Wansdyke, with its ditch on the north side running from Newbury across the Marlborough Downs to the Bristol Channel, is probably to be assigned to this period.

The struggle culminated in the battle of Mons Badonicus, fought some time between A.D. 495 and 503 (fig. 7). The Britons were victorious, and westward expansion of the Saxons was checked for over forty years.

This setback demonstrates the insecurity of the invaders. They were very much in the minority. Though it is difficult to assess the population of the province in late Roman times, there are grounds for supposing that it numbered upward of 1½ to 2 million. Even in the districts already overrun a large proportion of the population was of Celtic stock. At first the newcomers owed allegiance, as we have seen, to many tribal leaders who established local dynasties often at war with one another. Despite these ties, it is evident that the settlers regarded themselves more as Anglo-Saxons than as members of any local kingdom. They came to speak of themselves as belonging to the men who settled north of the Humber, *Nordanhymbrorum gens* (Northumbrians); or to the *Sutangli* (South Angles) who occupied the lands to the south of that river. This underlying sense

8. *Saxon "tun" or defended settlement. The long timber houses with their numerous out-buildings, stables and byres are protected by a wooden palisade and ditch.*

9. *Swearing allegiance at the coronation of a Saxon king.*

of unity greatly assisted in the fusion of the newly established Saxon kingdoms into larger confederacies, in the latter half of the sixth and during the seventh centuries.

From fourteen states there gradually emerged, with considerable bloodshed and strife, seven major kingdoms. These were Northumbria, Mercia, Essex, Middlesex, Kent, Sussex and Wessex. A fierce struggle against the native population appears to have taken place in the north when the Northumbrian kings extended their power to the west coast. Here the Britons applied to themselves a new name shared by their compatriots in Wales, Combrogies or Cymry, meaning " fellow countrymen ", embodying a spirit of national resistance still commemorated in the county name of Cumberland and in the Cumbries of south-west Scotland.

In the south the power of the West Saxons was extended to the Severn. Following the battle of Deorham (Dyrham near Bath) in A.D. 577, the three " chesters ", Gloucester,

10. Offa's Dyke, the greatest public work of the whole Anglo-Saxon period, consisted of an earth wall and ditch. It marked the western boundary of the Mercian kingdom, which achieved its greatest power under Offa II (757-796), and was probably constructed under the personal supervision of the king between 784-796. Well preserved sections can still be seen between Tryddan in the north and the Bristol Channel in the south.

Cirencester and Bath, were brought within the Saxon sphere of influence, and a wedge was effectively driven between the Britons of the south-west and of south Wales. Mercia expanded to the Welsh border, where the territorial boundary of Mercian power in the eighth century is still clearly visible in the remains of Offa's Dyke. This great earthwork once extended from the coast of North Wales to the lower Severn, and it was constructed by Offa II between 784 and 796.

The history of these major kingdoms before the Norman Conquest tells of the gradual shift of political power from north to south, from Northumbria to Wessex, and of the unification of the country under the royal house of Wessex.

11. *Many Celtic monasteries were founded along the coasts of Cornwall, Wales, Ireland and Scotland. The buildings included a church, a refectory and monks' cells.*

THE CONVERSION

Christianity had already made converts to the faith in Britain in Roman times. In the fourth century mention is made of British bishops attending church councils on the Continent, and an early church has been recovered in excavations at Silchester. Christian mosaics, wall paintings and symbols occur in a number of villas of the same period at Frampton, Chedworth, and in the rich man's house at Lullingstone in Kent. Small private chapels were also established in some towns.

Christian monasticism reached the Celtic West through such famous missionaries as St. Patrick in Ireland, St. Ninian in Scotland and St. Illtud in Wales. This was an austere and ascetic movement inspired by the fourth century desert hermits of Egypt, transmitted through the Gallo-Roman monastery of Lerinum (Lerins) off the south coast of Gaul.

The Anglo-Saxon settlers were, of course, pagan, and it was with the purpose of converting them that Pope Gregory sent St. Augustine to Britain in A.D. 597. King Ethelbert of Kent was converted, and churches and schools were founded in Canterbury (fig. 12). In A.D. 625 Paulinus, also sent by Pope Gregory, converted Edwin, King of the Northumbrians. Edwin, however, was killed in battle, and when his sons after a period of exile in the Columban monastery on Iona regained the throne, the Northumbrian church was placed in the charge of Archbishop Aidan from Iona, and became firmly attached to the Celtic (Scottic) branch. Two of Aidan's pupils, Cedd and Chad, preached Christianity to the Mercians and to the men of Essex. In Wessex, Bishop Birinus and his mission sent by Pope Honorius established a church at Dorcu (Dorchester-on-Thames) about A.D. 635.

The choice in favour of the Roman rather than the Celtic organization and practice

12. *Canterbury: the Abbey of St. Augustine. The original church of St. Peter and St. Paul founded by the Saint in 602 is at the extreme left.*

for the English church was made at the famous Synod of Whitby (A.D. 664), and it fell to Theodore of Tarsus, who came to Canterbury five years later, to implement this new policy.

During the ensuing century there flourished some of the greatest clerics and men of learning in western Christendom: Aldhelm (639-709) and Boniface (675-754) of Wessex, Cuthbert (625-687), Wilfred (634-709) and Bede (673-735) in Northumbria. As the influence of the church permeated society, thegns built their own churches, many, it may be suspected, the successors to heathen family temples, just as these

14. In the monasteries books transcribed in the scriptoria inspired the compiling of chronicles, histories, Lives of the Saints and other works, at first in Latin, then in Anglo-Saxon.

13. Late Saxon church tower at Earl's Barton, Northants, showing pilaster strips and arcading.

early houses of God became the forerunners of our parish churches.

In the north beautifully-carved stone crosses were also erected (fig. 15) at the base of which the word of God was often preached. At the head of the state the king became increasingly dependent upon the legal and administrative skill of his bishops and clergy.

15. *Ruthwell Cross: one of the finest Northumbrian crosses, it bears in runic lettering lines from the famous poem "The Dream of the Rood".*

Writing, in our modern sense, was unknown to the pagan Anglo-Saxons, though they possessed a runic alphabet of twenty-four letters. This was primarily suited to the inscribing of names or magic formulae on small objects of stone, wood, bone and metal ; indeed, an early poem advises all those who desire victory in battle to cut " runes on thy sword-hilt, on the hilt-ring, and some on the plates of the handle ". A few such inscriptions dating to before A.D. 600 have survived, being mainly personal names on weapons, such as spear-heads and knife or sword blades. More are known from the seventh and eighth centuries on coins, jewellery and other personal possessions. Longer quotations from poems and heroic verse are to be found on the Ruthwell Cross (fig. 15), and on the Franks casket, a whalebone box of Northumbrian workmanship now in the British Museum.

As among other primitive people, a rich oral literature flourished, particularly in the form of lyric poetry embodying the early myths of the Teutonic people, stories of their gods, the origin of their tribes, the deeds of illustrious kings as well as a good deal of vernacular knowledge expressed in gnomic verse including magic formulae and spells.

This epic verse was recited round the hearth in the great halls by professional minstrels to the accompaniment of a lyre or harp of the kind discovered in the Sutton Hoo ship burial. The popular appeal of such verse survived the conversion, and it is a reflection of the " Englishness " of the early Christian monks that they deemed it worthy to commit to parchment the epic verse of their heathen ancestors, admittedly now strongly tinged by Christian sentiment. What vicarious thrill did they experience in transcribing the epic tale of Beowulf, replete with the burning of feasting halls, the clash of arms and the terror of supernatural monsters ! What memories of the past were evoked by the poem *Widsith*, telling the adventures of a wandering minstrel at the courts of the migration kings. Perhaps the *Seafarer*, " feet fettered by frost . . . hearing nought but the sea booming and the cry of the gannet ", was identified with some distant ancestor who crossed the North Sea in an open boat. Like us, the industrious scribe probably pondered on which Roman town described in *The Ruin* presented its despoiled towers, gates and bath houses to the gaze of the early English settlers. The same pagan diction and metre appears in the verse of Caedmon and Cynewulf. In the earliest translations of the Bible the prophets and kings of the Israelites become mail-clad Saxon thegns, while Christ is depicted as a heroic prince.

Classical learning followed in the wake of the conversion. Many monasteries came to possess extensive libraries, first mainly of imported books, including the works of Virgil, Pliny, Ovid, Lucan as well as the historical writings of Josephus, Eusebius and numerous lives of the early saints. Because of their rarity they were industriously copied in the scriptoria " in letters of purest gold on purpled parchment and illuminated " like the famous Lindisfarne Gospels. Inspired by the classical world there soon flowed from English hands a stream of biographies, chronicles, letters and didactic works. A more practical application is to be seen in the mass of charters, laws, wills and other legal documents which now make their appearance in Latin, then in English. It is of interest to note that the cursive script used in Anglo-Saxon writing was not derived from contemporary sources on the continent, but would appear to have been inherited through the Celtic church from the fourth century Latin written in the Roman period.

TRADE

In the early period of settlement trade was limited, owing to the largely self-sufficient nature of an agricultural economy. Even so, there was a need for such basic commodities as salt and metals, both restricted in their natural distribution. Iron was essential to the manufacture of tools such as scythes, axes, ploughshares and other implements needed in wresting a living from the land, as well as weapons for its defence. Much of this traffic passed along the old Roman roads, still in a good state of repair, and along the main waterways. It was not long before certain areas gained pre-eminence for their produce — Cheshire and Worcestershire for their salt, Derbyshire for its lead, Essex and Berkshire for cheese, the sheepfarming uplands for their wool. Already during the pagan period a widespread trade developed in luxuries. Garnet-ornamented jewellery made in Kent was exported to Germany, possibly in return for Rhenish glassware, and African ivory and cowrie shells found in graves tell of even wider connections. English slaves were sold in the market place of Rome together with British hunting dogs.

Much of this early trade was carried out by barter, but in the seventh century Saxon kings (Eorpwald of East Anglia 616-628 and Penda of Mercia 632-654) struck coins based on Roman or Merovingian currency. The pendings struck by the latter king give us our modern 'penny'. Mints were established in many of the principal towns. In the later Saxon period international trade was principally in the hands of the Frisians, Jews and Arabs, the Frisians exercising control over the northern seaways, with trading colonies established in all the principal ports like London, York, Birka in Sweden, and Haithabu in Denmark. These merchants traded in silks, wine, weapons, English cloth, hunting dogs, ropes, amber, furs and slaves.

Contemporary documents are full of human interest, such as the story of the customs official who rode out to ask the business of the first Viking raiders to reach the coast of Wessex, and was killed for his pains; the account of voyages round the coast of Norway to the White Sea and to the east coast of the Baltic by Othere and Wulfstan in the reign of King Alfred; and the portrait of an eleventh century merchant in Aelfric's Colloquy: "I go on board my ship with my cargo and sell my goods and have precious things which are not produced here, and I bring it hither to you with great danger over the sea. Sometimes I suffer shipwreck with the loss of all my goods, barely escaping with my life."

16. *A lively trade developed with the continent and Scandinavia. Exports included English cloth, weapons, jewellery and other goods in exchange for silks, precious metals, wine and furs.*

His freight included silks, precious gems, gold, spices, wine, oil, ivory, copper, tin, sulphur and glass.

TOWNS

At the end of the Roman period many towns were abandoned, never to be inhabited again until modern times. The early Saxons had no tradition of building in stone, and many Roman structures were readily allowed to fall into decay. The majority of towns, including London, however, recovered after a period of collapse, emerging as important market or trading centres in the later Saxon period.

That extra-mural settlements were common is indicated by the continued use or extension of established Roman cemeteries. Where later rebuilding took place the new streets meandered between the mounds and hummocks of fallen debris, as may be seen in the street plans of Colchester, Gloucester, Winchester and other ancient cities.

The same story of economic decay and abandonment applied to the numerous villas and farms in the countryside, which was still a lonely place, with widespread tracts of almost virgin forest, heathland and fen. The main river valleys abounded in extensive marshland, the haunt of thousands of wildfowl. Few villas remained in occupation other than by squatters, the newcomers preferring to establish their homesteads and villages on lands cultivated by the Romano-British peasants and on the heavier soils of the main valley systems.

The character of these early settlements is revealed by place-names. Those ending in -*wick* often denote a building in the mead or hayland of an earlier settlement ; -*stead* or -*fold* indicate more outlying buildings while -*ton* implies an enclosed agricultural settlement defended by a stockade. Recent discoveries in the Welland valley and elsewhere have shown that the farmsteads were similar to the rectangular timber frame dwellings in the continental homeland. The smallest with sunk floor and wattle and daub walls served as weaving sheds or the homes of serfs and dependants. In the royal townships, such as Yeavering in Northumberland dating to the seventh century or in the royal ' palace ' at Cheddar (fig. 18) established in the ninth century, the main hall is surrounded by smaller rectangular buildings. At Yeavering one such structure served as a pagan temple. Close by a timber grandstand resembling the trinagular *cuneus* of a Roman theatre may have been used as the meeting place or moot of the local assembly (fig. 17). It is tempting to

17. *In the 7th century tiered timber stands were used at places of assembly. It was probably before such a stand that Paulinus preached Christianity to the Northumbrians at Yeavering in 625.*

imagine Paulinus preaching to the pagan Northumbrians as recorded by Bede from this small platform facing the tiered benches.

Following the conversion many towns sprang up around the monasteries, at staging posts along the roads, and at market places. With the onset of the Viking invasions King Alfred made provision in Wessex for the fortification of important centres. The additional security thus provided in a troubled age further attracted traders and craftsmen, who swelled the ranks of the middle class burgesses and guilds. The burghal system was influenced by the current practice in the Danelaw. Here the Five Boroughs of Lincoln, Stamford, Leicester, Derby and Nottingham served both as military garrisons and trading centres. Each had its own " law men ", was governed by a Jarl or Earl, possessed its own army and was defended by a palisaded earth wall and ditch. With the reconquest of the Danelaw English burhs were established with their own garrisons on the Danish model, the surrounding military and administrative districts emerging as shires.

With the return of more peaceful conditions in the tenth century trade expanded rapidly. Street names — Fishmongers Street, Shoemakers Street, Tanners Yard — still reflect the bustling life of the period. At Thetford in Norfolk part of the industrial quarter of a late Saxon town has been excavated, to reveal a mass of timber and wattle and daub houses, workshops, kilns and rubbish pits between straggling streets leading past numerous churches to the town centre and the principal ford across the river.

18. *Saxon Cheddar: view of royal palace site founded by King Alfred. The enclosure contains the royal hall, a small chapel, mill and various domestic buildings.*

20. *Saxon agriculture: heavy ploughs were drawn by teams of oxen. Other implements included scythes and sickles.*

VILLAGE LIFE

The daily round, except in the more prosperous households, was a hard one for women, who were expected to milk the cow, prepare food, salt or dry stocks for the winter, brew ale, and help in the fields, as well as spin and weave. In fact, life afforded little relaxation for anyone, except in the winter months when the working day was shortest. Heroic tales were then told by professional or local minstrels to the accompaniment of the lyre or harp round the open hearth. In every village one or more of its members was well versed in heroic legends and folk tales.

Time was reckoned in the Roman way, the hours being counted from our 6 a.m. The main meal was taken at the ninth hour (*none* — noon), our three p.m. The cow, ox, sheep and pig provided meat for the table, as did hens, geese, ducks and wildfowl. Fish abounded, and fruit was plentiful. Honey was used for sweetening.

19. *Saxon village surrounded by arable strip fields and common land beyond.*

21. *Interior of Saxon hall: after feasts minstrels recited heroic lays.*

22. *The Minstrel.*

23. *Weaving and Embroidery.*

Indoor pastimes included a form of draughts, but games of chance rather than skill were popular, as is evident from numerous bone dice and counters. During the Viking period Arabic traders introduced the game of chess from India.

Outdoor sports included hunting, hawking, fowling and snaring, as well as horse riding, horse fighting, and bear baiting. The training of young men as warriors included such exercises as wrestling, swimming, jumping, and playing ball games.

Embroidery was a favourite occupation among women of the nobility.

24. *Hawking.*

25. *Wrestling.*

A BUNGAY, SUFFOLK   B RAINHAM, ESSEX
C FAVERSHAM, KENT D UPCHURCH, KENT   E KEMPSTON, BEDS.

26. Glass in Saxon times; A, pouch bottle; B, drinking horn;
C, palm cup; D, jar; E, cone beaker (Roman), F, King Alfred's jewel.

ART

In common with other primitive peoples the early inhabitants of the
European forests and plains evolved art styles based upon simple geometric
patterns which could be readily incised on pottery, wood, stone and metal or woven
into a variety of fabrics ranging from basketry to cloth and wearing apparel. Intricate
patterns of great beauty arose in the portrayal of writhing animals on weapons and
ornaments. The art of the Anglo-Saxon jeweller survived the conversion and achieved
European renown in the ninth century, though it is now permeated by classical and
Celtic influences. One of the most beautiful examples to survive is the jewel ordered to
be made by King Alfred (fig. 26). A similar fusion is to be seen in the illuminated manuscripts and books compiled in the monasteries, such as the Book of Durrow and the
Lindisfarne Gospels of the seventh and early eighth century.

After the Viking wars in the late ninth century monastic life revived, and with it
English manuscript art achieved another period of greatness, this time under Carolingian
inspiration best exemplified in our own Winchester School. (fig. 27)   In the tenth and
eleventh centuries an impressionistic style of drawing became popular, with spindly
figures and swirling draperies quickly drawn but of great vitality.

Though references occur to carved wooden idols in the pagan period none has survived.
The symbol which banished these ancient gods triumphed in numerous stone crosses,
particularly in the Celtic west and in Northumbria. One of the finest examples is the
Ruthwell Cross in Dumfriesshire with beautifully engraved Christian scenes and vine
scrolls on the shaft and portraits of the evangelists on the arms of the cross.

27. A page from the Benedictional of St. Aethelwold, the richest example of the art of the
Winchester School. 10th century.

28. *Many monasteries, including Lindisfarne, Jarrow and Iona, were pillaged and sacked by Viking raiders.*

THE VIKINGS

At the end of the eighth century England was again subject to raiders from Scandinavia, this time crossing the North Sea in fine clinker-built ships with high masts and strong sails from Norway as well as Denmark. At first the raiders came merely to prey upon the rich and comparatively peaceful communities who, weakened by internal political factions, were totally unprepared for such incursions from the far north. Many ports and monasteries along the coasts were ruthlessly plundered — Lindisfarne in 793, Jarrow the following year, Iona in 802 and 806. In the wake of the Norwegian raiders there followed a stream of settlers who were to establish an earldom in Orkney, flourishing colonies in the Western Isles, and kingdoms in the Isle of Man and Ireland. Not only have the graves and hoards left by the early marauders been recorded, but the farms and

settlements of the colonists have come to light. Their houses were not built of timber but of stone and turf, the forerunners of the crofts in the Scottish Highlands and Islands.

The rectangular farmsteads contained two rooms — kitchen (eldhus), and living room with a long stone lined hearth and lateral raised platforms on which the benches and beds lined the walls. Byres were attached to the main building so that cattle wintered under the same roof. Close by were the smithy, outhouses and serfs' quarters. The

VIKING ROUTES

////// DANELAW
:::::: NORMANDY

SCALE OF MILES
0   100   200   300   400

30. *The Vikings established many thriving communities. The coastal villages were important fishing centres, small boats landing catches of cod, haddock, saithe and ling which were wind-dried, smoked, or salted before being sent to the larger towns and villages inland.*

29. *Interior of Viking farmstead with earth floor, and long stone-lined hearth flanked by raised dais for tables, benches and beds. The kitchen was at one end, a byre for cattle at the other.*

settlers grew corn on arable strips close to the settlements and kept sheep, cattle, pigs and ponies. Wool was carded and spun before being woven on upright looms into a rough cloth known as waḋmal. Fishing was the mainstay of many coastal settlements, and perforated stone sinkers occur of the type used in line fishing. From such farms and settlements emigrants were destined to sail to Iceland, taking with them many Celtic serfs, as described in the Laxdaela Saga and other Icelandic family tales.

40

In south-west England an interesting village has come to light at Mawgan Porth in Cornwall. Though it dates to the Viking period (850-1050), it reflects the western extension of Saxon influence noted earlier rather than any Viking intrusion. On a hillside overlooking a shallow bay a hamlet was established consisting of several groups of stone-built houses with turf roofs, built around small courts. Cattle were stalled at one end of the principal buildings. At the other end were the living rooms, with central hearth and box beds ranged along the walls. The villagers collected shellfish, fished in the bay, and herded cattle. Iron was in use, but most of the surviving implements are of

31.   *Mawgan Porth: a small hamlet with courtyard houses dating to the 10th-11th centuries. The graveyard is on the slope above the settlement.*

stone or bone.   The cooking pots had holes for suspension over the fire, their leather thongs being protected by clay lips.   Higher up on the hillside was the small cemetery, in which villagers were buried in stone-lined coffins.

To the east, armies of Danish Vikings were ranging the English countryside by the middle of the ninth century.   Danish supremacy was established in the Danelaw, which incorporated the old kingdoms of Mercia and Northumbria, while Wessex was under severe pressure from this Viking power.   The defeat by King Alfred of the Danish forces at Edington and the conclusion of the Treaty of Wedmore in 877 proved to be the

32.   *A room in one of the Mawgan Porth courtyard houses.*

33. *Trelleborg: about 1200 men could be accommodated in this large camp of the late Viking period in Denmark. It consists of a circular military encampment surrounded by an outer bank with wooden palisade and ditch. In the inner camp sixteen boat-shaped houses were arranged in groups of four in each quarter. Another group of houses was located in the outer court.*

turning point in this Anglo-Danish struggle. From that date the Viking settlers in northern and eastern England were gradually brought under control, the process culminating in the unification of the country under Athelstan (924-939). Following his death, however, English fortunes again declined, and the country was conquered by the Danish kings Sweyn and Canute at the beginning of the eleventh century. For a time these kings ruled an empire extending from the shores of the Baltic to the Scilly Islands. It was

44

probably during this period that the great military camps such as Trelleborg, Aggersborg, Fyrkat and Odense were established in Denmark, with a possible outlier at Warham Camp near Wells in Norfolk.

On the death of Canute's son, Harthacnut, this empire collapsed, and the English throne was regained by Edward the Confessor of the House of Wessex, who had grown up at the court of the Dukes of Normandy.

It was only natural that Norman influences should be widely felt at his court, just as French institutions came to affect the church, the law and civil administration. Edward, however, died in January 1066 at Westminster, and his council decided that he should be succeeded by the most powerful noble and soldier in the land, Harold, son of Earl Godwine, and not by his grand-nephew the young Edgar Atheling. Harold's brief reign of nine months was beset by family strife, and overshadowed by the constant threat of invasion. His brother, Tostig, who had been stripped of his earldom of Northumbria, landed with a fleet of over three hundred ships in the Humber, only to be defeated and killed by Harold at the battle of Stamford Bridge on the 25th September.

34. *Trelleborg: The large houses had bow-shaped sides and were surrounded by colonnaded verandahs. The roads were formed of wooden sleepers.*

35. Death of Edward the Confessor.

THE NORMAN CONQUEST

Three days later, William of Normandy, whom Harold had once promised to help gain the English throne, landed at Pevensey, and the English army hurried south to meet this new threat.

The events leading to the invasion, and to Harold's death at the Battle of Hastings, are portrayed, as in a series of film stills, in the famous Bayeux tapestry. The scenes so vividly presented provide a storehouse of information about life in the eleventh century. It is our best authority for the arms and armour of the period, as well as providing valuable information about ships, the building of fortifications, houses and wearing apparel.

The Norman conquest of England was an event of European importance, for it deprived the Scandinavian kingdoms of a strategic base on the maritime flank of Europe. Without it the Vikings ceased to threaten western Christendom, and England, after vacillating between Scandinavia and continental Europe for over two centuries, was drawn within the sphere of medieval French and Latin culture.

PAST AND PRESENT

The heritage of the Saxon period is all around us, in our language, laws, church and administrative system. Each recalls in no small measure the history of those turbulent centuries between the collapse of Roman rule and the coming of the Normans. It is not surprising that the period between 400 and 1066 has been called the most formative in the history of the English speaking peoples.

To the archaeologist the half light of the period presents an immense challenge, for, despite documentary sources, place-names and visible remains, much has been swallowed

36. *The Norman Conquest: the landing of the Norman fleet at Pevensey in 1066.*

up by the earth. In recent years the redevelopment of land has opened up the soil and offered unprecendented opportunities to examine archaeological remains buried for centuries. Strenuous efforts have been made (and continue to be made) to recover this evidence now threatened by total destruction.

Already a rich harvest has been gleaned, including the royal township or palace sites at Yeavering, Old Windsor and Cheddar, extensive cemeteries of the pagan and early Christian periods in Kent, East Anglia and Wessex, as well as Saxon levels at Canterbury, Hamwih (Southampton), Thetford and London. Individual farmsteads and small settlements are coming to light in the west country. In Scotland the most extensive Viking settlement yet discovered '' west-over-sea '' has been recently excavated at Jarlshof. The discovery of the Sutton Hoo ship burial in 1939 indicates what immense, if rare, treasure may yet be found in English soil.